Merry Chris

Hope you think
this book is
interesting
    Love
    grandma

ON
READING
PALMS

Prentice-Hall, Inc.   Englewood Cliffs, N. J.

ON READING PALMS

by Peggy Thomson

illustrated by Dale Payson

Printed in the United States of America • J

Prentice-Hall International, Inc., London
Prentice-Hall of Australia, Pty. Ltd., North Sydney
Prentice-Hall of Canada, Ltd., Toronto
Prentice-Hall of India Private Ltd., New Delhi
Prentice-Hall of Japan, Inc., Tokyo

Book design by Dann Jacobus

Library of Congress Cataloging in Publication Data

Thomson, Peggy.
    On reading palms.

    SUMMARY: Introduces the art of interpreting the signs and patterns of the hands.
    1. Palmistry—Juvenile literature. [1. Palmistry] I. Payson, Dale, illus. II. Title.
BF921.T46   133.6   73–17296
ISBN **0–13–634246–9**
ISBN 0-13-634253-1 (pbk.)

Special thanks to Dr. Michale E. Keeling of the Yerkes Regional Primate Research Center, Emory University.

4

"Wilson began to study Luigi's palm, tracing life-lines, heart-lines, head-lines, and so on, and noting carefully their relations with the cobweb of finer and more delicate marks and lines that enmeshed them on all sides; he felt of the fleshy cushion at the base of the thumb, and noted its shape; he felt of the fleshy side of the hand between the wrist and the base of the little finger, and noted its shape also; he painstakingly examined the fingers, observing their form, proportions, and natural manner of disposing themselves when in repose. All this process was watched by the three spectators with absorbing interest, their heads bent together over Luigi's palm, and nobody disturbing the stillness with a word. Wilson now entered upon a close survey of the palm again, and his revelations began."

Mark Twain

For

the young and old
who lent a hand

TABLE OF CONTENTS

Introduction

Look at your hands—right hand, left hand, front and back. Useful things, hands. Useful for carrying packages, tuning a carburetor, pulling a sled or petting a pup.

Your fingers tell you if something is smooth or prickly, gooey or rough.

Look some more at your hands. At the strong lines that cut across your palms. At the web of fine, wavy lines—close together—that cover your skin from your wrists to your fingertips.

Look at them and think: Is there a mystery about them? Are hands mysterious as well as marvelous? Do they have a tale to tell? Secrets to unfold? News—about you?

Could it be possible to "read" your hands—the way you read a map or a book?

In the past some people thought this might be so. Some think so still.

Hands painted on the walls of caves and hands carved on stone, thousands of years old, tell without words that early men and women must have looked at their hands in wonder the way you look at your hands now. Chinese people, Indians from India, North

American Indians—all studied their hands and tried to puzzle out the mysteries.

What about the lines that show on every hand but on no two hands—not even twins' hands—exactly alike?

Why is it some people have few lines and some have so many? Why do the lines on some hands look clear and neat, while others, criss-cross, run this way and that? It would make sense for the lines to come from use, from folding and unfolding the hands many times. But people who work with their hands seem to have fewer lines—not more—than those who don't do manual labor. And right hands often seem to have fewer lines than lefts.

Long ago people came to think the lines on hands might be signs. They might tell about your mind and heart—your personality.

The art of reading the signs in hands came to be known as palmistry, just as reading the signs in stars is known as astrology. The two went together. Palmists named parts of the hand with the names of stars. People with unlucky signs in their hands were "star-crossed;" people with lucky signs were in tune with the stars.

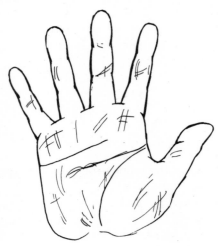

People saw patterns in their hands; they liked to think it showed a pattern in their lives. Some also wanted it to tell their future, to solve the biggest mystery of all: What will happen in ten years, or tomorrow?

People looked into their hands for signs that tell the future, just as they looked to the stars and to the patterns of tea leaves in the bottom of a cup, and smoke and clouds in the sky. They also looked for those signs in dice and in cards, even in a chicken's insides.

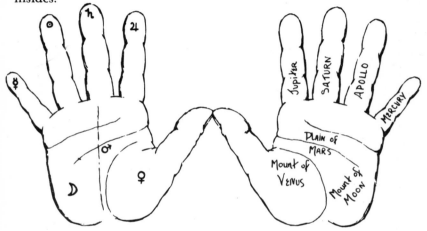

People look for signs like that still. They find it reasonable and exciting and fun. Have you seen, by a country road or in a city window facing the street, a big picture of a palm? And the palm has a question mark on it? It's an advertisement for a palmist, someone who reads palms for money. Many of these palmists are cheats, promising to tell the future for your cash. In England it's against the law to read palms for money—or even for free. In some states here it's illegal, too.

On the other hand, hundreds of millions of people in Asia do believe deeply in palmistry, as they do in astrology. They rely on their readers of signs just as Americans need the help of auto mechanics.

Most palm readers tell you they can't read the future and would not if they could, though some insist it may be possible and many say they can read your past. Most of them read your palm for the pleasure of telling you what they can about you and surprising you with things you may not even know about yourself.

You can learn to read palms, too.

Thinking back, do you remember how you learned to read? How you learned that marks on a page stand for sounds? A curvy snake line for an S? S-P-O-T for spot? You learned to look at the print on a page and someone taught you a system for translating it.

Palmists have worked out a system for you to use—though they don't always agree—a system for WHICH line means WHAT. In fact there's a map of your hand with a special geography.

Answer one question first. Now, before you know anything more about it, do you think there is something to palmistry? A lot to it? Or nothing at all?

Sailors on long trips, in the times sailors chased whales, used to read hands as a way to pass the time. Many people today think of palm reading in just that way—as a pastime, a game. Some call it silly. They say the lines on hands all have to do with how the skin and muscle and bone are joined and how they work together.

Study your hand. Read it as you learn how to—from this book. And then see if you think the same.

The feelings hands give you are part of what palm reading is about. A limp hand feels lazy to you. A wet-rag sort of hand makes you wonder if its owner is worried or sick. As a palm reader you look at hands and remember them. You store them in your mind. And then when you read a new hand you have a whole collection of hands to compare it with.

Active, lively hands, even at rest all look like they could peel apples or chop wood. Nervous and fidgety hands are always drumming and tapping, opening and closing. The hands of people deep in thought look quiet while other hands are floppy. Some are fluttery, flying this way and that. Some hands always seem to be fists, tensed, clenched and mad.

In the middle ages palmists read the left hand because it was closer to the heart. Today people read the active hand—the hand that writes and holds tools. If you are right-handed, check back to the left to find out the potentials you were born with. If you're left handed, it's the other way around. Your active hand shows what you are making of your life.

About Thumbs

Your thumb can be your beginning—not because it's the logical place to begin but because a thumb is so definite. Palmists agree the thumb is one of the most important signs in your hand.

The thumb tells a lot about character. First joint (with the nail): willpower. The second joint: reason. The first joint is usually just a little shorter than the second.

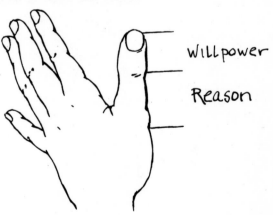

Willpower

Reason

With a long, strong thumb you will make the most of your talents and abilities (it takes the rest of the hand to tell you what *they* are). Count a thumb long if it reaches past the end of the palm, maybe as much as halfway up the joint of the first finger. A long second joint says you are reasonable. You give everyone a chance. You are loyal and fair. You never let down a friend. Your advice is good. With such a thumb you practice the trumpet or the oboe until you play it well. To stay on the swimming team you train every day. You write and re-write until words say what you mean. You are not a quitter. When you set out to fix a bike, you finish. If your doctor says "no chocolate" you give up chocolate cake.

With a very short thumb, you are short on will, short on reason. You may like music and poetry but you don't want to work at them. You are glad to help out but don't want to be in charge. You are a good companion, easy to get along with. You hope problems will go away without your having to do anything about them. You have trouble making up your mind, though once you do you are stubborn. You don't plan. You act fast and think later. You think about your family and friends but you are not much interested in the rest of the world.

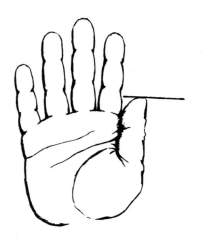 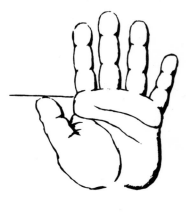

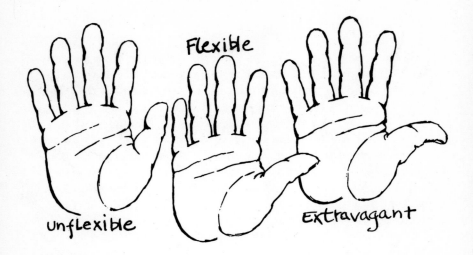

Flexible

Unflexible

Extravagant

Now test how flexible your thumb is. If its tip doesn't bend back at all, you are an unbending, inflexible person. You don't want to give in. You pick an argument. And you are stingy. If it flexes slightly, you are open to reason, and you are tolerant and fair and generous. If it is very, very bendy, arching way back, you are generous to the point of being wasteful and extravagant. People like to have you around because you are so agreeable. You will do what people want you to do in order to avoid an argument or an unpleasantness. The trouble is, you try so hard not to lose your temper that when you do lose it, you lose it badly and get quite wild.

Check your thumb *angle,* too. Hold your thumb naturally: is it close to your hand or out at a wide angle? If your thumb angle is very small, if in fact your thumb seems to bend in toward your hand, then you are close-mouthed and secretive. You keep back what you think. And you are selfish. You are narrow-minded and opinionated. If your thumb angle is small but your thumb doesn't bend in, you are somewhat cautious and timid. You don't like change.

If your thumb angle is wide, a good 45 degrees, making a big V, you are open-minded, generous. You are independent. You can handle change. But look out if your thumb angle is huge. The

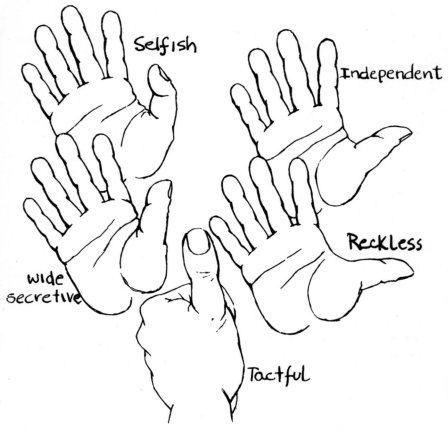

Selfish

Independent

Reckless

wide
secretive

Tactful

bigger it gets—the more generous, the more independent, the more you don't care what anyone else thinks, the more reckless you are. The good thing about you is that change is a breeze to you. If you move, you get used to your new home fast and you make new friends easily.

See if your thumb has a waist, a nipping—in, at the second joint. If it does, you have tact. You say just the right thing to make people feel good about themselves. You have a way with animals, too. If the first joint is full and round though, you are more straight-talking and frank. If it is really very thick, then you say things that hurt people's feelings.

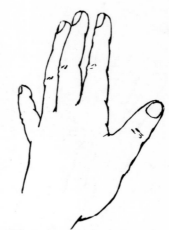

A very thick inflexible thumb with a square tip can mean you get violent. You hit and smash.

A very short pointy thumb can mean your are fickle. You blow hot and cold with friends.

A very flat nail on your thumb means you get cross if you don't have outdoor exercise.

Is there a chain instead of a straight line across the base of your thumb? Aha! In an argument—I did, you didn't, yes I did —you like to have the last word.

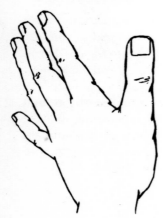
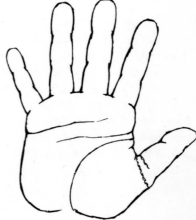

Introducing Fingers

I   Put down your hand—on a table or a lap—just naturally, when you're not thinking about it?

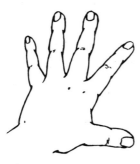

• Fingers wide apart? A sign you are open and generous. You like giving to people. You give things and ideas. You show your feelings.

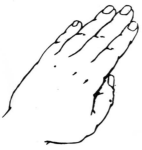

• Fingers closed? The thumb maybe even tucked inside? You are careful in what you say and do. You keep many thoughts and feelings to yourself, guarded like secrets.

19

II When you hold the fingers of your right hand in your left hand and bend them backwards, how bendable are they?

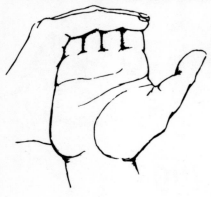

- Almost not bendable at all? You are unbending yourself, a stiff person. You don't welcome new ideas or a change of plans.

- Quite bendable? You are an interesting person, reaching out to understand ideas and feelings. Quick to grasp them, too.

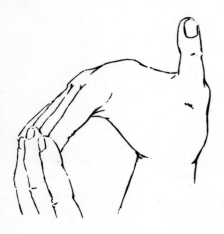

- Extra-bendable? You are "far out," so original you stand out.

III When you press your right palm between the thumb and fingers of your left hand, how does your palm feel?

- Soft, almost spongy? You like comforts. You have a quick mind. You dream. (Does your thumb say you make your dreams come true?)

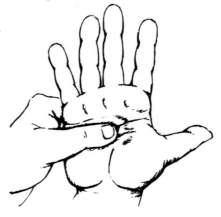

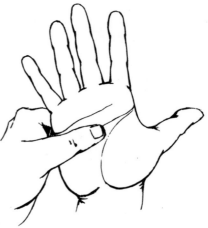

- Springy like a hard rubber ball? You put energy into your actions and your thinking.

- Hard? You shut other people out. Your energy goes to hard physical work. You don't change your ways. You are stubborn.

IV   When you close the fingers of your hand tightly and hold up your hand, do you see light through the spaces between your fingers?

• If you do, money slips through your fingers. You lose money or spend it easily. The spaces also mean you have a curious and inquiring mind. You like to ask questions.

Believe It Or Not

A funny thing palmists point out about the size of hands: it is often people with small hands who like to deal with large problems and large ideas. They run large businesses and make large plans. They sign their names with over-size signatures. And it is often people with very large hands who do fine, careful work, with attention to tiny details. Large hands write their names small. They set diamonds into tiny claws for rings. They repair watches or fill teeth. Check your dentist's hands and ask him what he thinks.

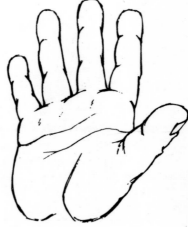

Palms and Fingers

Now look at the shapes of hands. This is difficult, and your conclusions depend on many things. This is why a palm reader can spend an hour or two reading a single palm.

In general, there are square palms and long palms and each of these has long fingers or short. You can take square to stand for action and long to stand for thought—which is some help, even though you know it's not so simple as that.

Here are some *clues* to keep in mind when you're looking at shapes of hands.

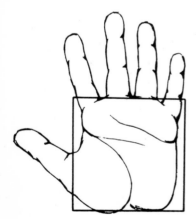

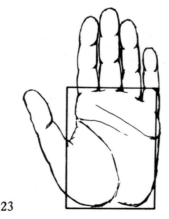

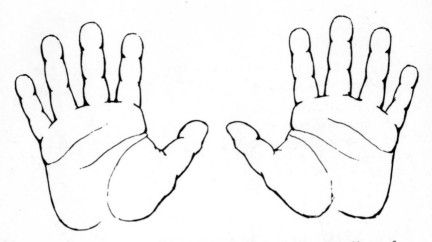

- Short fingers speed up thinking. You get the big outlines of an idea, decide quickly, act fast.

- Very short fingers speed up thinking to carelessness.
  You rush out the door with one sock blue and one black.
  You glue a model together before you read the directions.
  You get mad at ideas you don't understand.

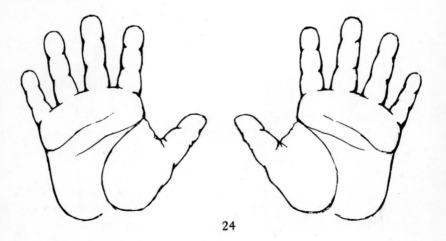

- Long fingers slow thinking down. You plan, make lists, look at all sides of a question.

... Knots on knuckles slow thinking down even more. You measure exactly—1¼ is not 1½ to you. Misty weather is different from moist.

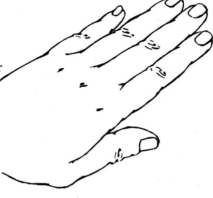

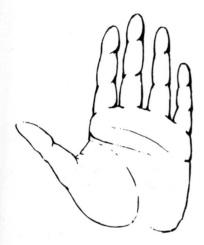

... Pointed fingers show good imagination, keen "radar."

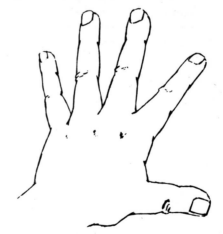

... Square fingers show reason. You won't be pushed around.

The hand with the *square* palm is the action hand. The hand of a do-er. You like to work hard, especially if you can do it out of doors. You have a good feeling for nature. You like to produce things with your hands—carrots, chairs, clothes, a new roof. You have good sense and a level head—not silly. You obey rules. You don't pick fights. There is nothing tricky about you. You have a strong sense of what is right. You are a loyal friend. When you have a problem you don't fret about it. You face it, decide what to do, and you do it.

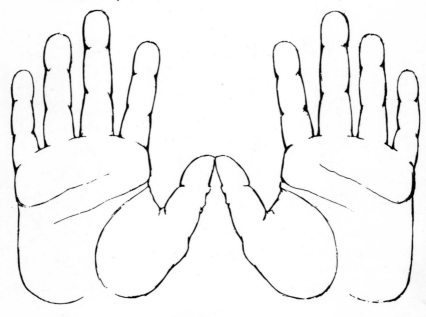

That's a square hand with average-length fingers. (Looking from the back the longest finger is about the same length as the palm. Or you can tell by folding your fingers down to your wrist. Long fingers will almost reach. Short fingers will stop just past the middle of the palm.)

Now picture that square hand with very short fingers, very stubby, and it is the sign of a law-and-order, meat-and-potatoes, no-nonsense person—who may be solid to the point of being obstinate and unimaginative.

Picture the square palm with long fingers. Here the hardworking, down-to-earth person is a thinker as well, with a logical mind and a good eye for detail. You enjoy working problems out. With that combination you make a good craftsman or sportsman, lawyer or doctor.

Now add knotty knuckles to the long fingers on the square hand, showing you like to work in a system, inside a set of rules. You do well in science, math, music, library work. Those fingers are right for a surgeon, who has to think out every move before he cuts.

27

A *long* palm with short fingers is often a high energy, "fiery" hand, especially if it has a spatulate, or spade-shape in the palm and in the fingertips. The fingertips spread out like little digging spades. That shape always means energy. You are an exciting person with drive, power, go. You like lots of quick movement and travel and change. You follow where your strong interests lead; you don't worry about the opinions of friends. You don't wait around for slow people or listen to the end of long arguments. You may be an inventor or an explorer.

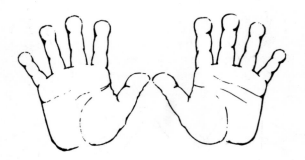

The long palm with long fingers—about as wide at the fingertips as at the base of the palm—is the philosopher's hand. It probably has knotty fingers, too. You are the person who likes to ask why. You talk well but only when you have something to say. You save your money. Your old shoes will do. You make a good teacher, historian, writer. Lincoln had a hand like yours.

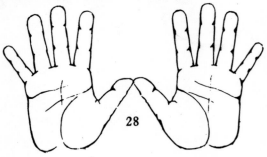

If your long palm with long fingers gets thinner at the top, tapering almost to a point, like an upside-down cone, then you have a sensitive hand. You have a strong imagination. You are very much open to feelings of all kinds. You love parties, but you also worry a lot. You're a pleasure to be with. You enjoy people— and music and art and the stage, but the rest of your hand will have to tell if you have the drive to work at the arts.

If you can't decide which shape you have, you can say you are an interesting mixture—with many possibilities.

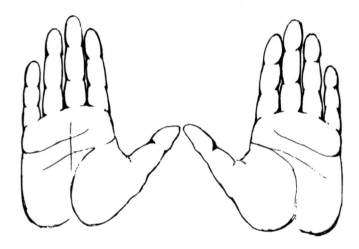

Fingers and Fingernails

Fingernails and the shapes in which they come:

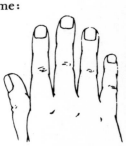

• Wide—you argue and complain

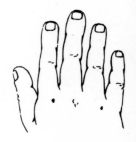

• Short—you are logical, reasonable

30

• Long—you are understanding, tolerant

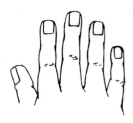

• Extra narrow—you hide your feelings

• Long with squared-off top and bottom—you demand facts

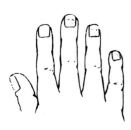

Nails with ripples or ridges
are signs of a worrier.

Each finger has its own story to tell. And here you get the special names that come from astrology.

The first finger is Jupiter and has to do with ambition. The second is Saturn, wisdom. The third is Apollo, gifts in the arts, style, flair. The fourth or little finger is Mercury, which has to do with your quick wits.

Saturn is bound to dominate your hand since it's in the middle and slightly longer than Jupiter and Apollo. It's a sign of a nicely balanced nature if Jupiter and Apollo are about equal in length. It's a sign you are confident, sure of yourself in a comfortable, quiet way.

There are certain signs that give added strength to the significance you've found in the fingers. Check to see if you have an unusually long, strong finger. Notice if any pads—palmists call them mounts—are outstanding. Do any of your fingers lean toward another?

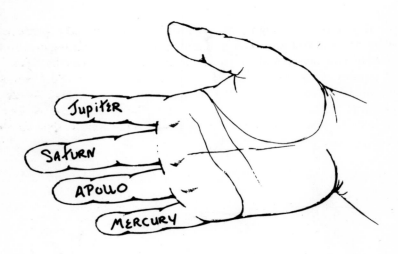

Imagine a line dividing your hand from the tip of Saturn down to your wrist. The thumb side of that line is the active side of your hand—the power and doing side. The little finger side of your hand is the passive side—the listening, sensing, dreaming side. Do you notice a slant of your fingers one way or the other?

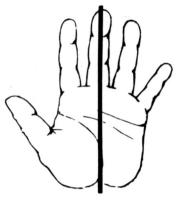

If *Jupiter* is straight, you are ambitious. You take pride in what you do, you are a natural leader. You have a strong sense of honor. You are proud of your family and a trustworthy friend. If Jupiter is almost as long as Saturn, you are bossy. You expect people to do what you say. If Jupiter is short, shorter than Apollo, you want to follow rather than lead. You don't like responsibility. It may be you aren't sure of yourself; it may be you just don't want to push yourself forward.

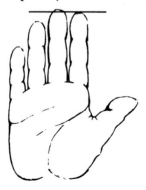

A waist on the third section of Jupiter, near the palm, means you are a good cook.

Saturn stands for a love of knowledge. A long straight Saturn says you are a deep thinker, serious about life. You enjoy time alone outdoors. If Jupiter and Apollo both lean to Saturn, you don't like partying. If Saturn is knotty as well as long and the Mount of Saturn is high, you may become a famous scholar but you will have trouble changing a light bulb or remembering where you left your bike.

If the tip of Saturn is spade-shaped, you like science. If Saturn is heavy in the third joint, you may have a green thumb.

A bend in to Saturn is the collector's sign—you like to own things.

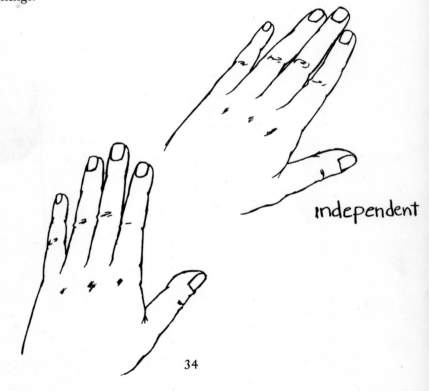

independent

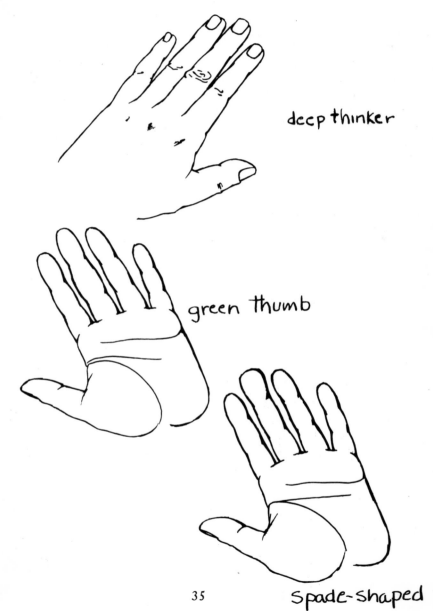

deep thinker

green thumb

spade-shaped

Apollo is the important finger for performers. With this finger you are moving from the thinking-side of the hand to the feeling-side. A straight Apollo finger reaching halfway up the first tip of Saturn shows it's easy for you to show your feelings to other people. You can be gay, exciting, funny for your family or friends or for an audience. If Apollo is almost as long as Saturn and longer than Jupiter you want to hear approval and applause; you long for glory. If your thumb is long and strong besides, you will work at your artistic gifts. If it's a short thumb you may be content to have beauty around you—to hear fine music and see color and shape in artwork and buildings and nature.

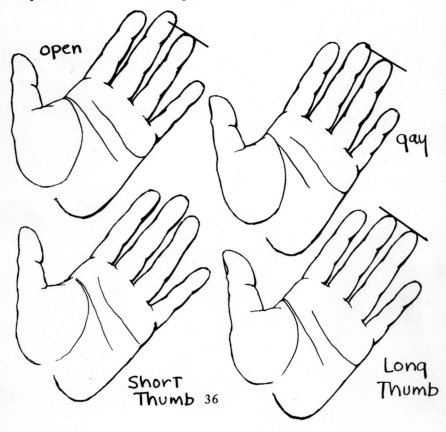

open

gay

Short
Thumb 36

Long
Thumb

A spade-shaped fingertip on a strong Apollo finger—long or short—is a sure sign you can be a success on the stage. Look for lines, called "whorls," on your fingertip and on the Mount as well—signs you are original enough to have your name in lights!

If Apollo is so long that it passes the tip of Saturn, you are a gambler—excited about taking a big risk.

Up-and-down lines on the Mount of Apollo:
• three lines—you will always have money
• more than three—you are a jack-of-all trades. You sing a little, dance a little, play the flute a little, but don't try to be tops at any one.

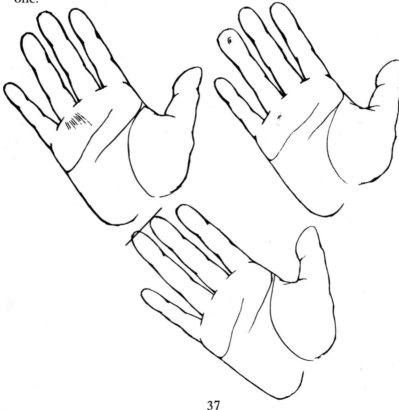

Is *Mercury* long? Then you are quick with words, clever at games and puzzles, quick to understand people. You make money easily. Your guesses and hunches are often right. A long pointy tip is a sign you love words. You are a big talker—and a gifted singer. A long square tip means you make speeches and argue well. A long spade-shaped tip means you excite your listeners with fiery speech.

If Mercury starts low in your hand, well below the starting line of your other fingers, then you are shy. A person with a short little finger and a solid mount is jolly.

If Mercury is extra-long, up to Apollo's nail, and a bit crooked besides, you are so clever you are fiendish. You like to trick people.

A little finger bent out away from the hand is said by some to be the sign of a good ear for music; by others it is a sign of difficulty in getting along with people. Sculptors and architects have little fingers that are rectangular and blocky.

Up and down lines in the Mount show you will do well as a doctor or nurse; you are good at making decisions.

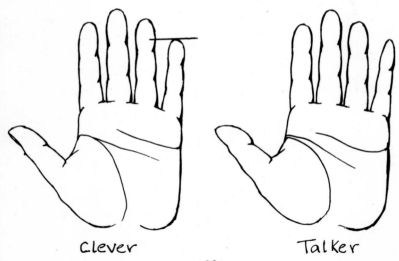

Clever   Talker

38

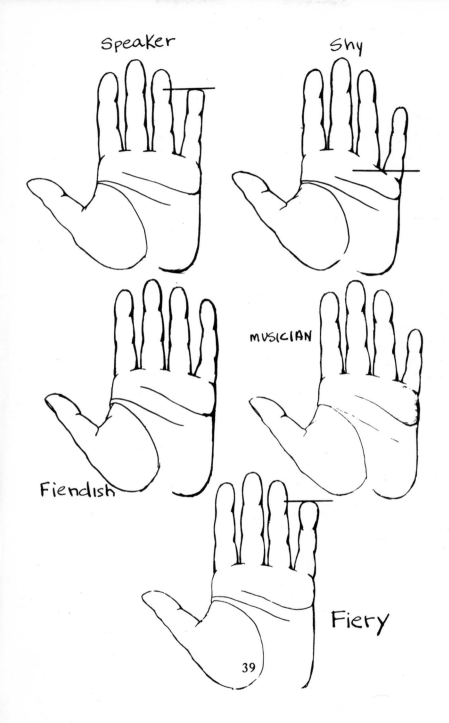

Speaker

Shy

MUSICIAN

Fiendish

Fiery

39

MOUNTS

In a young person's hand the mounts don't show up as well as they do in an adult's. High mounts or firm high padding in general have always been taken as the sign of a "lucky hand." They show you have lots of drive and confidence in what you can do.

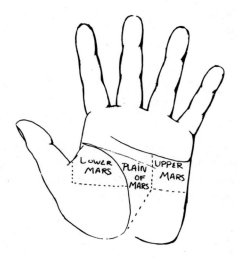

You will see the *Mounts of Upper Mars* and *Lower Mars* on your "map." Both have to do with fighting—your fighting spirit (not just in war but in argument) and your will to fight—physically. And you will see the hollow of your hand called the *Plain of Mars.* If the hollow is very deep you are timid and you back down in an argument. If it is gently hollowed you are even-tempered and confident. If it is flat, not hollowed at all, you have so much spirit you take chances even when there's no need.

A whorl on your Mount of the Moon is a special sign of imagination. With a square hand you may be a fine craftsman.

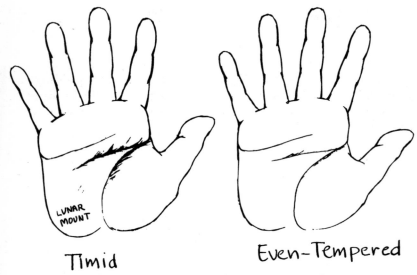

LUNAR
MOUNT

Timid   Even-Tempered

The *Mount of the Moon,* or *Lunar Mount,* covering the lower outside area of your hand's map, is the mount of imagination. A firm bulge here is a sign of your love for art and travel. If the edge of the mount bulges out to the side, you are drawn to the sea.

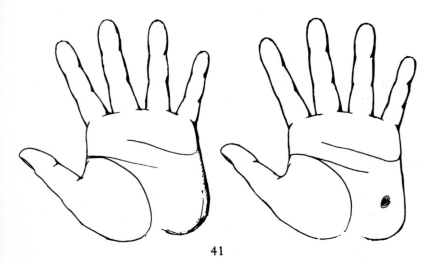

The *Mount of Venus* is really the third joint of your thumb. If it's round and solid, you are a loving, generous, hugging sort of person, with a gift for song and melody. You show your love for family, home, fellow men. Rays running across the mount from thumb to palm are signs of special warmth. A knob or sharp angle at the thumb's second joint shows a good sense of rhythm.

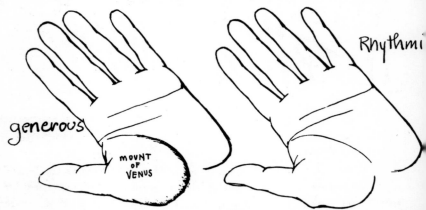

generous

Rhythmi

MOUNT
OF
VENUS

If Venus is very high you are wasteful. You spoil yourself and your friends. If it's flat you are friendly and patient with people, appreciative and fair—but cool. You keep your distance.

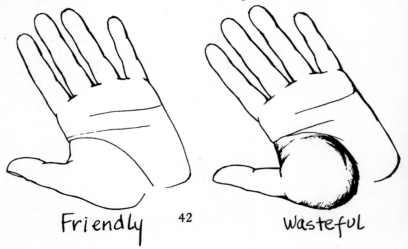

Friendly   42   wasteful

Hand Lines

Now that you know your hand geography, the lines can tell you a tremendous lot. You can be definite about the direction they run. You can plot where they start and stop.

You will find that long hands tend to have more lines than square hands (though many poets have square hands well covered with lines). Women tend to have more lines than men. The passive hand tends to have more lines than the active one.

Not every line is found in every hand, though a famous reader of palms says he has never heard of a hand without a Life Line. Lines do change. Some lengthen. Some appear for the first time. Some disappear. A patchy tangle on a mount may sort itself out to a tidier pattern.

Lines that run even and clear are nice signs. They just suggest by the look of them a smoothly running life. Lines that are chained and feathery, broken and tattered-looking get where they are going, too. They just suggest a few side trips and lumps along the way.

Deep lines go with strong feelings, very definite likes and dislikes.

The Fate Line, which is missing on many hands, often appears on children's hands for the first time between the ages of eight and twenty.

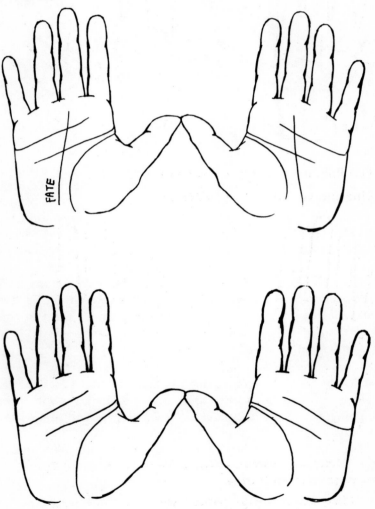

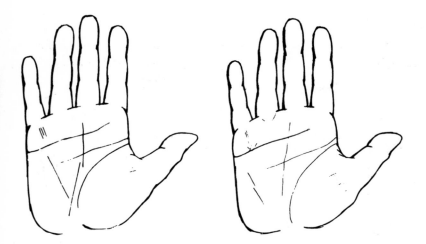

Few lines mean energy is more physical than mental.

Fine lines go with finely tuned senses.

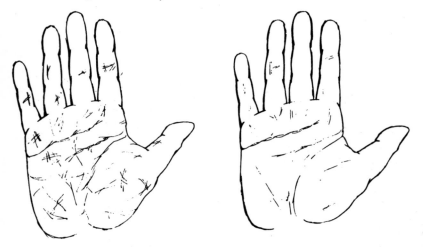

Many lines in a tangled web mean nervous energy that is scattered and tiring.

Many lines in clear pattern mean nervous energy well used, under control.

Palmprints

The best way to study lines is to make a hand print—a messy but satisfying business. You will need: black ink (oil-base works better than water-base but stains won't wash out), a roller, glossy paper, (erasable typewriter paper works well) and a rubber pad or sponge.

Press about half an inch of ink from the tube onto a metal cookie sheet and roll it back and forth with your roller until there's an even film. Be sure your hand is very clean and dry. Then you roll the ink directly onto your hand. (You don't put your hand on the cookie sheet.)

Place the rubber pad under the paper to make the surface springy rather than hard. Roll your hand down flat, putting the thumb to the paper last. Use your free hand to press down the hand you are printing. If the hollow of your palm won't print, if it shows up as a white hole, then fold a paper towel into a wad and place it under the center of your paper to give a little bulge. Ask a friend to hold down the paper while you get your hand unstuck and lift it off. You will probably have to bungle a few prints before you know how hard to press. If you're impatient, you can press your hand—one section at a time—on a cloth covered ink pad. Your own print can be the start of a collection. As you do the hands of your friends for them, make an extra copy for yourself.

The three main lines that stand out in almost every hand are the lines of Life, Head and Heart.

The *Life Line* is your energy sign. It can't tell you if you'll live to be 100, so there's no point in looking for news like that. In fact palmists don't agree on which end of the line to call the childhood end and which to call old age. If your Life Line is strong, even and clear, then you are a high-energy person, full of pep, ready for anything. If it's thin or wobbly or short you coast along at a comfortable pace. Breaks along the Life Line mean changes— good and bad. Many fine lines running through the Life Line indicate you are a worrier.

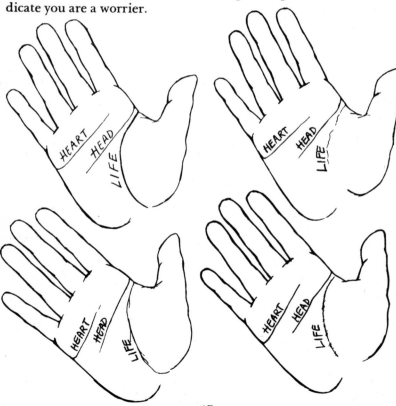

If your Life Line makes a wide curve into your palm, that, too, is a sign of vigor. You are rugged and outgoing. You seek adventure. If your Life Line hugs close in to your thumb, then you're a calm, quiet type. A line that curls back around the base of the thumb is a sign you will always stay in very close touch with your family no matter how far apart you are.

If your Life Line starts high, on the mount of Jupiter, then ambition rules your life. You are always off and running; you like to get ahead and like to win. If your Life Line branches off toward the end and strikes out for the Mount of the Moon, you may move some day to a far distant place.

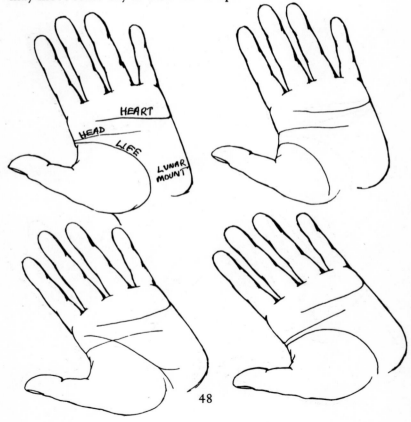

The *Head Line* tells about your mind—not your IQ score but the quality of your mind. If your line goes straight across your hand, right to left, like a ruler line, then you have a cold logic. You are interested in facts and prices. A Head Line that bends takes in many new ideas.

A high Head Line that curves down slightly shows talent for math and sciences. This is the line for builders, designers, lawyers. The line with a strong downward curve is the sign for writers, poets, filmmakers.

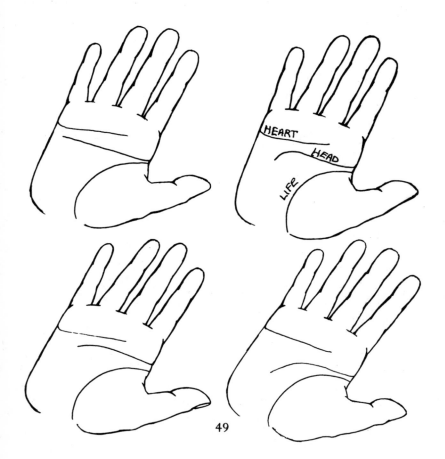

The downward curve carries the line into the Lunar Mount, which you know as the home of imagination. If your Head curves downward you play with facts, re-arrange them, come up with something surprising and new.

If your Head Line drops sharply down to the lower corner of the Lunar Mount then you live in a world of your own.

If your Head Line is short, stopping below Saturn, you have a one-track mind. If your Head Line curves up, to Mercury, then you put your wits to work for one thing especially—and that's money.

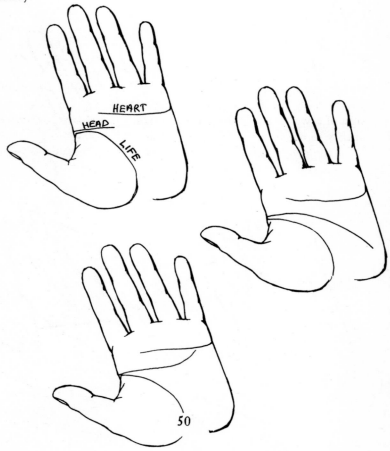

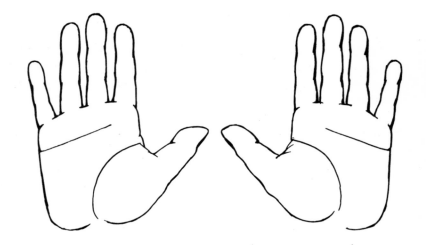

A faint Head Line may mean it's hard for you to concentrate. Either you would rather be doing seven other things, or your worries interfere. A chained Head Line? Most palmists say that, too, is the sign of a wandering mind; but some say the chain strengthens the ability to concentrate. Take your pick!

The long, deep, clear-running Head Line is easy to interpret: concentrate and put your wits to work for you.

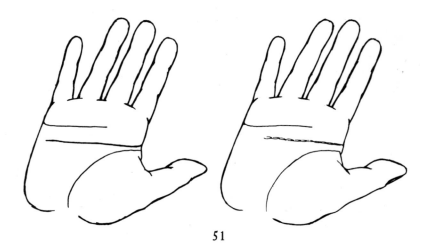

The *Heart Line* tells about your affections. The strength of the line shows how you feel about people—not just one special person, but people. If you have a strong Heart Line you have strong affection for family and friends, for people you read about, for strangers.

If your Heart Line slants up, toward the space between the Mounts of Saturn and Jupiter then you are a warm-hearted person indeed. A deep and true friend. If your line runs high onto the Mount of Jupiter (ambition, remember?) then you are rather particular about the people you love. You expect them to measure up to your ideal. If your line forks on Jupiter you are extra lucky and happy in your affections. But if the line goes all the way across your palm it means you need to be told over and over, that others care for you.

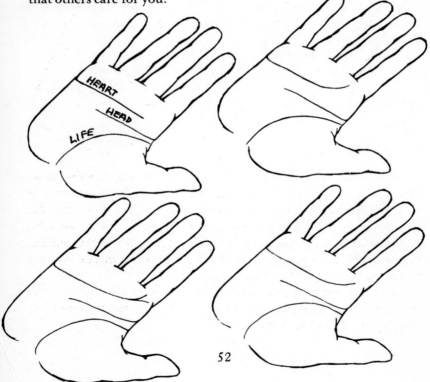

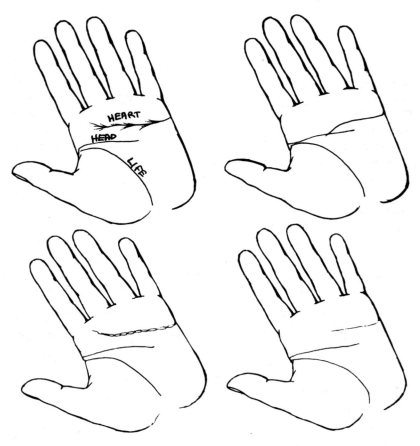

The Heart Line with many little lines running from it shows you are always in love, flirtatious. Some say the upward-running lines are happy romances; the downward-running lines the disappointments. The Heart Line dipping down to the Head Line under Saturn means you are possessive rather than warm-hearted. You want to own people. A chained Heart Line means you are fickle, changeable in your affections.

If your Head Line is short or faint then you are a calmer sort of person. You are slower to take to people, less apt to show your affection for them when you do.

Like snowflakes, there are no two palms alike. The unique relationship between your headline and heartline tell you something.

A space between the starts of Head Line and Life Line is a sign of independence. You think for yourself and act on your own. You don't wait to see what other people think or do. If the space is wide rather than narrow, then, look out, you are quick and impatient. Your independence is close to recklessness. If the two lines join at the start then you are cautious by nature. You do pretty much what is expected. You learn to become independent; it isn't just natural to you. If your lines join for a long way, then it takes you a number of years to become independent.

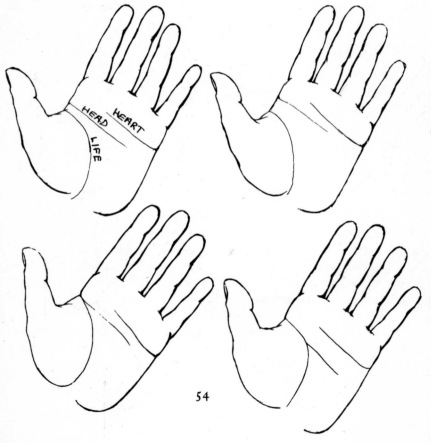

Some people have a Heart and Head line that is all one line, called the Simian Line. They are pretty unusual, emotional people with big ups and downs.

It's a good sign to have a fairly wide space between the Heart and Head Lines. The space is a sign of your tolerance. You understand people and get along with them even if they are very different from you. If the two lines are crowded, close together, you don't think much of "outsiders."

Look for a deep space between the Heart Line and the fingers. It's a sign of strong sympathy. You put yourself in another person's place. You feel with the Olympic winner; you feel with the loser. You laugh with people but you don't laugh at them or tease.

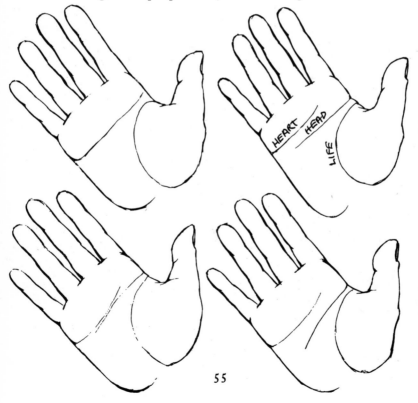

55

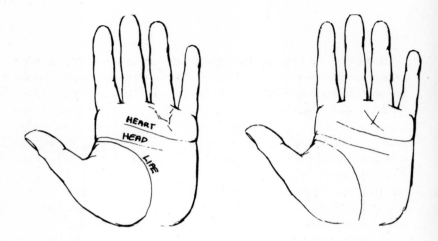

- *Girdle of Venus*, a V-shape line below Saturn and Apollo, above the Heart Line is a sign you are keenly sensitive, high-strung, emotional. If the line is broken you are a bit too much so for your own peace of mind.

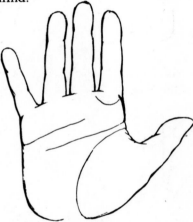

- *Solomon's Ring*, an arc on the Mount just below Jupiter, is a rare sign. Do you have it? Then you have a gift for seeing deep into yourself and understanding people. You are fond of the mysterious. Palmistry appeals to you!

- *A Line of Fate* runs up through the palm in many hands, on a more or less straight line from the wrist to Saturn. If it forms a nice triangle with the Head Line and Life Line, it's considered a lucky sign.

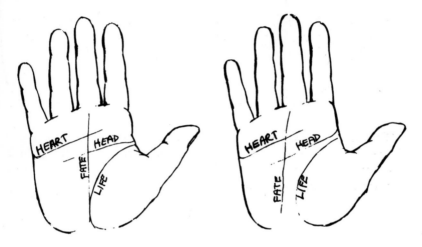

- *Stars* are success signs. On Jupiter, personal success and a happy marriage. On Apollo, fame on the stage!

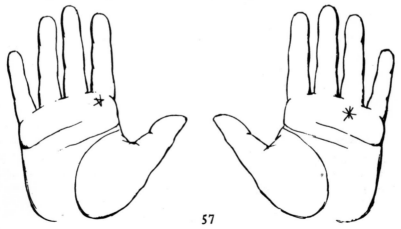

Fingertips and Fingerprints

159, 599, 644

The FBI (Federal Bureau of Investigation) has 160 million fingerprints on file in Washington, D.C. And the almost unbelievable
fact of the matter is that, truly, no two are exactly alike. As with
snowflakes and leaves and zebra stripes, nature does not repeat
itself.

And yet all fingerprints are very much alike. There are only
three basic types. The patterns of the tiny skin ridges on the tips
of your fingers are either whorls or loops or arches in different
variations. Because there are so few types, the FBI can file a new
set of prints—yours for example—in with the 159, 599, 644 it already has, as neatly and exactly as you would tuck a new word into
the dictionary.

The patterns on your fingertips were formed five months before you were ever born. Though the ridges and the spaces between them will keep growing as you grow, they never change
with age as other parts of your body change. They stay exactly
the same. No wonder fingerprints have been, for almost a hundred
years, the tool for identifications.

Look at the enlargement of a single loop-type print. It is
marked for 25 details—starts, stops, branching—by which it can
be told apart from every other loop print in the world. And think

of the unfortunate criminal who had his fingerprints cut away and new, smooth skin from his side grafted in their places—only to find he could be identified by the pattern of skin ridges on the other joints of his fingers.

You have patterns covering your palms and covering the soles of your feet. You probably left your footprint on your birth certificate. Have you ever seen it?

All other primates in addition to man have the patterns, too—apes, lemurs, monkeys. In fact spider monkeys, woolly monkeys and howlers, who hang by their tails, have ridges along the underside of their tails as well. On hands or on tails those ridges, finely formed and mysterious to see, serve to prevent slipping. They give a good grip. And they give a good sense of touch—for exploring by feel.

Many scientists have studied this "friction skin." There are people as well who do whole "readings," of character, based on the print of a single thumb. There are old Japanese formulas for reading what one whorl means in a hand or five or nine or ten.

Whorls stand for individuality and originality and restlessness. The Japanese say they are the sign of talent in handicrafts.

Loops stand for ease in expressing yourself, open-ness, flexibility.

Arches for stubbornness and keeping secrets.

Tented arches for high-strung emotion, an ear for music, an eye for art.

You will need a sharp eye—and a magnifying glass—to see what you have. Your parents' may be quite different since fingerprint types are not inherited.

Appendix

Which Friend Is Which?

Susan and Alexa are friends, though they say they are both so strong-willed they sometimes get on each other's nerves. In some ways, including size, as you can see, they are quite different. Try matching each girl's description with her print.

Susan is on the student council and directs student plays. She sings, paints, writes poetry, plays the piano (and likes competitive auditions). Although she's not athletic, she likes team games. People bring her their problems, and she likes to listen and to analyze, hoping one day to be a psychologist. She likes cooking for her younger brothers and sister (her specialties are breakfasts and banana splits). She's a good, steady student and wants to have lots of "best" friends, not just one.

Alexa is clever, witty, excitable, impulsive; she loves to discuss and argue and wants to be a criminal trial lawyer "defending people I think are innocent or have good reasons to be guilty." She does not hold offices or join clubs at school. She likes to party or shop or cook candy with friends but spends a lot of time listening to music and reading. She has ups and downs in mood. Though ten is her bedtime she often reads on after midnight. She's a good student but admits she is a little lazy.

Alexa is below
Susan is above

62

63

Look Alike Twins

Twins James and David are not identical twins but have hands that look very much alike, as if they could belong to the same pair, with long tapery fingers and a fine web of lines criss-crossing the palms. James is left-handed, and David is right-handed. To a palmist, the boys' hands spell out thoughtfulness, warmth of heart, sensitivity, a tendency to be critical of themselves, to brood, to worry over little things, and very unusual powers of intuition—that is, they sense things (see the marked Girdle of Venus) without being told in so many words.

As babies the twins did communicate with each other in a special language no one else understood; when one was ill in the hospital, the other at home moped and wouldn't eat. Today the twins are constant companions. They play hard, like to fight and laugh together. They eat all the time and are always thin. They get almost exactly the same grades and make the same scores in basketball and pingpong. Though they're well-liked, they claim to be shy and very quiet at parties.

A palm reader, looking just at the prints and not seeing either boy, says James's heart line shows him to be the more fickle of the two (liking someone very much one day and cooling off the next) and David's shows him to be the more loyal and easy-going. The palmist didn't say anything about James's temper. (Did he not see a sign of it? Or was he being tactful?) But both boys recognize it as a fact of their lives.

David says "James can stand up to bossy kids better than I do." James says, "Yeah, some people I don't care if I hurt their feelings." James is faster with a fist, altogether more outspoken and claims he can out-yell his friends.

BUT—do you notice that David has a space at the start of his head and life lines—the sign of an independent nature—but James's head and life lines join? Is that a contradiction? Or is it possible that David, who according to friends and family and the twins themselves is the gentler and quieter of the two, is also the more independent?

64

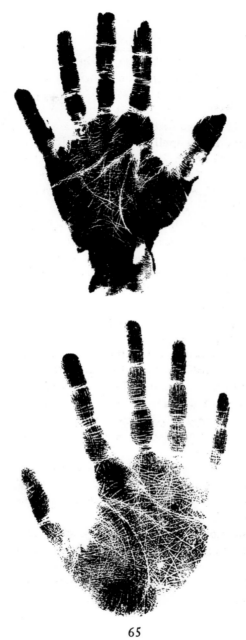

65

A New Hand And An Old One

Stanwood, age 92, has been reading other people's palms for pleasure for more than 60 years, and he thinks his own palms are good indicators of his life and character. His is the hand of the thinker—it is neither broad nor thick—but it has signs of the man of action, too. The fingers are medium in length and have strong endings—not just squarish tips indicating a strong personality but the spatulate or spade-shaped tips indicating a vigorously sure-of-himself person who doesn't care a hoot for other people's opinions and will carry out his ideas and plans against any opposition.

At first glance the head line is the most noticeable feature. It is unusually long and clear-cut, slanting down toward the mount of the moon—the sign of a strong intellect with a bent toward creative imagination—and with a fork at the end, which he calls a sign of writing ability. In fact Stanwood has run a very unusual school and written many books and is still writing.

The wide space between the head line and the start of the life line means independence in thought and action. He has that. And though his life line looks weak about midway he has a parallel "defense line" in toward the thumb, as a strengthener. (Stanwood still weeds his garden and shovels his snow.) His heart line, which was short, indicating a lack of deep affection, may fit with the fact that he waited until he was 38 to marry. His intuition line, the Girdle of Venus, is growing too, in his right hand to match the very strong one in his left hand. And he feels this is happening just as he is learning to tap his intuitive powers more than before. He says "Once the idea comes to me, my books write themselves."

Baby

Baby "VW" has a tiny soft hand compared to Stanwood's heavily lined one, but his principal lines are clearly marked—as they were when he was born—and by coincidence they are even very much like his. The baby has a rather short heart line and a strong headline sloping toward the lunar mount and the same very unusual feature of a "defense line" running parallel to the life line, in toward the thumb. VW, with his squared fingertips (showing he is not to be pushed around,) is not an easy subject to handprint. His skin is moist, and his fingers like to clutch rather than to stay out flat.

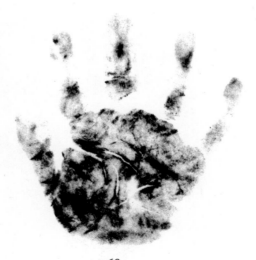

Index

About The Author

Peggy Thomson, free lance magazine writer and mother of three, says she reads her hand to say she is cautious and only moderately open to new ideas. "The age-old idea of palmistry was certainly new to me. I first liked it because it involved children in the close observation of their own hands and in talking about what they saw and recording and analyzing according to a system. Now I've come to like the system. It's neat and exciting." Has she become a believer? She didn't say.

About The Artist

Dale Payson is a believer, and has been since she had a palm read when she was a teenager. Her palm reveals that she is imaginative, good with her hands, shy and has a good ear for music. A palmist once told her that she has a long life ahead of her, which she plans to spend traveling (she's already been around the world), drawing and painting.